£2-50

Who ma
Land \

A Study in the Landscape
Archaeology
of Somerset's North Marsh.

by
Keith S Gardner

A Pennant Special
for
Nailsea & District Local History Society
5 The Perrings, Nailsea BS48 4YD

ISBN1-900722 04 3

Frontispiece   **A *Bow* over the Blind Yeo.**

CONTENTS:
Abstract.

List of ILLUSTRATIONS:

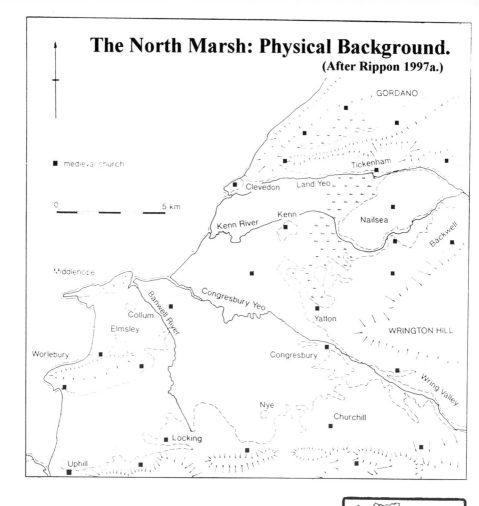

The North Marsh: Physical Background.
(After Rippon 1997a.)

GORDANO

■ medieval church

Tickenham

0   5 km

Clevedon   Land Yeo

Kenn River   Kenn

Nailsea

Backwell

Middlenope

Congresbury Yeo

Banwell River

Collum

Yatton

WRINGTON HILL

Elmsley

Worlebury

Congresbury

Wring Valley

Nye

Churchill

Locking

Uphill

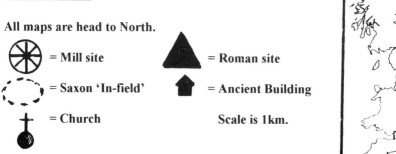

Key to Maps:

All maps are head to North.

⊕ = Mill site   ▲ = Roman site

◌ = Saxon 'In-field'   ⌂ = Ancient Building

✝ = Church   Scale is 1km.

Fig.1

STUDIES in the NORTH MARSH.

ABSTRACT. *In the peat and clay wet-lands of the northern part of Somerset's North Marsh, (bounded by Clevedon, Wraxall, Flax Bourton, Backwell, and Claverham, and to the south by the Congresbury Yeo), virtually all the drainage and passage of water is via a system of waterway channels cut or amended by the hand of man over the centuries. This review is not intended to be an 'in-depth' study but rather an outline survey to demonstrate the potential for further work in the field of Landscape Archaeology.*

1.   INTRODUCTION.

1.1   Archaeological and historical studies in Somerset's central and southern wetlands, with their Prehistoric trackways and Iron Age lake villages, have very much overshadowed the potential significance of similar studies in what was traditionally known as the North Marsh. **(Billingsley 1797)** **[Fig.1]** Even **Williams (1970)** hardly touched the surface of these moors bounded by the villages of Banwell in the south, Clevedon in the north, and Nailsea and Congresbury to the east. Recent research however by Dr. Stephen Rippon of Exeter University has demonstrated Romano-British (RB) use of much of the clay lands for agricultural purposes during the 2nd to 4th centuries AD. **(Rippon 1997a p.81-91)** The purpose of this paper is to present an outline summary of recent field studies on the post-Roman drainage systems, in the hope that it will serve as a basis for further historical and archaeological research into their origins.

1.2   The depressed sea levels of the last Ice-age allowed drainage lines to develop from the Carboniferous Limestone massif of Mendip and its north-western outliers to points of entry into a pre-Flandrian sea, estuaries which have long since been buried by the deposits of the post-Flandrian marine transgressions. Nevertheless many of the original streams are still draining the higher grounds but, left to nature, lose their direction if not their identity when they reach the barrier of the marshland. It is then that the hand of man has been brought to bear in determining their onward passage to the sea, effecting drainage in times of flood and irrigation in times of drought.

1.3   The purpose of wetland control is to:
a)   keep the tidal salt water out.
b)   let the hill drainage pass through the marsh and control it's exit to a low tide outfall.
c)   dispose of surface rain water as necessary .
d)   store the surplus fresh water during tide-lock or drought, and
e)   irrigate the water meadows.

2.   The DRAINAGE SYSTEM.

2.1.   One indication of the antiquity of the system is the preponderance of Old English terms still in traditional use, (and their erroneous use by modern authorities !) Surface rain water is channeled from the fields by *gripes* (land drains) giving the surface a corrugated effect reminiscent of ridge and furrow. Some of these are demonstrably as early as Romano British in date **(Gardner 1985 p.17) (Rippon 1994, 1995, 1996, 1997)** and resemble RB farm plans on the adjacent hills **(Gardner 1977 p.161-174)**. Their relationship to subsequent field features provides a sequential date if not an absolute one. Gripes drain into the *rhyne* system of open ditches perhaps 1 - 2 metres in width and the whole network of these, many of 18th/19th century Enclosure period, are controlled by sluice gates or *clyce* which can be raised or lowered, draining land as required. The rhynes becoming progressively wider eventually drain into a *yeo*, often via a *gout* and it is important to note that Yeo was the word FOR a main waterway and not the name of a particular river. Rivers if named take on a local possessive, eg Banwell River, or Kenn River (not River Banwell etc.) To complete the glossary a *bow* is a bridge and not a bend in the road as mapmakers and road authorities would now have us believe. The final requirement is controllable access to an estuary where the ebb tide level is lower than that of the outfall. This is effected through a *yere* (an archaic spelling but preferable to a *year* or an *ear* as the Ordnance Survey confusingly insist.) A yere is once again a form of sluice or hatch allowing water to flow out but not in, and has the same linguistic root as 'weir'.

2.2   The whole system is supported by sea-walls, some of which have been advanced in order to enclose areas of reclaimed land, leaving earlier sea-walls inland. Other *"walls"* exist in apparent isolation inland, often serving as causewayed roads, but originally intended to divide one moor from another preventing local flooding, or diverting or separating main drainage systems. Three such names are in current use, Nailsea Wall, the Gang Wall, and the Meer Wall; the Banwell river is bounded by a wall and the existence of others must lie hidden in the archives as did the Wow Wall **(Coward 1980 pp151-158).**

2.3   Maintenance work on the combined system was a communal responsibilty often involving parish church wardens in the 15th century, and later Juries of Dyke Reeves under a Commissioner of Sewers. Ditches were *'thrown'* and *'keetched'* to keep them clear, the final responsibility on farmland being the owner who was in turn responsible to the Dyke Reeve. The work was measured in a linear manner in *ropes* (20 ft.) or *lugs* (5 1/2 yards - the rod or *land yard* basis of acreage)

3.   GEOGRAPHICAL LOCATION.

3.1   The **NORTH MARSH** is now bounded on the western littoral by a series of sand-dunes accumulated on the coastal clay belt in the same way as the South Marsh is protected by similar features at Berrow and Brean. From Uphill to Worlebury and from Worlebury to Middle Hope no major drainage line flows through the dune system, the clay belt water draining eastwards and appearing to force the Banwell River northwards to its estuary in the north-west facing mud-flats which run from Woodspring to Clevedon. These mud-flats are now surmounted by sea-walls, (qv 2.2 above) two lines of man-made barriers between which the accumulated *warths* lie at a slightly higher level than the older land behind the inner sea wall. At Kingston Seymour there are still a few of the dole-stones marking the maintenance responsibilities of landowners in proportion to their acreage protected by the wall.

3.2   These sea-walls are breached (under control) by the drainage lines originating in the limestone hills to the east and south. There are three main systems. The northern has a west flowing system which takes the line Barrow Gurney via Wraxall and Tickenham's peat moor to Clevedon. Most of this flows directly to sea but some water drains into the central Yeo which originates on the north slope of Mendip, passing via Blagdon, Wrington, Congresbury and Wick St.Lawrence . This divides the North Marsh into two with the southern moor draining northwards from Banwell via St.Georges to Woodspring although complex works divert much of the water to the estuary of the central Yeo.

3.3   For the purposes of this paper it is proposed to review only the system north of the Congresbury Yeo, ie Clevedon with Wraxall, Backwell, Nailsea and Tickenham, and Yatton with Kenn.   [Fig.1]

4.   `The CLEVEDON YEO Complex.

4.1   The moors south of Clevedon are currently drained by three **YEO** systems; the **LAND Yeo,** an artificial embanked contour channel, the **MIDDLE Yeo**, the ostensible lowest natural course and the **BLIND Yeo**, i.e. blind in the sense of a blind alley with no outlet.

4.2   The western end of the oolitic Cotswold outlier Dundry Hill, is drained by a number of brooks, most of which head north east to drain the Ashton vale acquiring such names as Colliters Brook and Ashton Brook. However a series of springs in the area of the Barrow "tanks", (reservoirs) |os.i.| form a brook which flows through Barrow Gurney westward to its apparent outfall at

Clevedon. For the sake of clarity we shall refer to this as the **BARROW BROOK** although the OS show it as the Land Yeo. **[Fig.8]** In Barrow its power is utilised by three mills with their leats. It then meanders through the walled enclosure of the Romano-British site at Gatcombe **(Branigan 1977)** [os 2.] whence its course has been manipulated to serve three more mills, Gatcombe and Kincott, (both in Long Ashton), and Bourton mill, before passing on to drive yet another mill at Watercress Farm, Wraxall **(Bodman 1994)** .[os.3] **[Fig. 7]**

4.3 Superficially it now becomes the LAND YEO, meandering to the north of Wraxall House mill [os.4] along the valley to Jacklands Bridge [os.5] **[Fig.6]** and as an obvious embanked contour stream via the mill at Tickenham [os.6.] to enter the sea at Clevedon Pill [os.7] **[Fig.2]**

4.4 500 metres west of Jackland's Bridge a number of springs give rise to a series of westward flowing streams including the MIDDLE YEO, and the PARISH BROOK. both of which eventually drain across the peat **[Figs. 3-5]** and through the clay belt into Clevedon Pill. Whilst these all drain around the north of Nailsea 'island' a further stream, the KENN RIVER, flows from near Watercress Farm around the south side and enters the sea at Kingston (or *Sutte*) Pyll [os.8] to the south of Clevedon, with an overflow stream, the YATTON (or Little) RIVER draining to the CONGRESBURY YEO [**Fig.9**]

10

5. The PROBLEM:

5 .1 All the above is reasonably apparent from a most cursory glance at the Ordnance Survey map. What is not so obvious is the effect that the hand of man has had in creating most of these waterways, digging, blocking, embanking, diverting, with the greatest problem being 'who did what when?' The problem begins where the 'Barrow Brook' leaves its reasonably well defined valley and enters the flat plain between Wraxall and Flax Bourton at Water - cress Farm. This plain is level enough to have permitted a delta-like internetting of various streams if unrestricted by levees.

5.2 At the foot of the Failand Ridge, (the Carboniferous limestone hill which extends from the Avon Gorge to Clevedon) lie a series of springs, three of which add significantly to the local drainage problem. North and north-east of Watercress Farm is the first group of springs which immediately combine to form a brook running westwards to pass north of a wood known as Wamballs or the Little Wood. Local field names include Wambrells *(et var)* but whether derivation or source the stream is locally called WAMBLES or the LITTLE RIVER. **[Fig.7.]**

6. The MIDDLE YEO:

6.1 Left to its own devices the natural course of this Little river, which now owes nothing to the Barrow brook, (although it may have done in the pre Land Yeo era) would run the length of the shallow valley at its lowest point, and perhaps justifiably be referred to as the infant Middle Yeo.

It would originally have passed the (? mill) pool on the south side of Wraxall House, its course being marked by a stone bridge in the middle of a field 550 metres SE of Wraxall House.[Fig.6] From here it crosses the road and would continue westwards along the hedgeline south of Birdcombe Court were it not for the fact that it merges at the road with the LAND Yeo, which has come around the other mill on the north side of Wraxall House. Its natural line would join with the second of the spring outlets, (on which was based a Mesolithic settlement), **(Sykes 1960pp.106-122) (Gardiner 1998)** and join its flow east of the Trout Farm at Jacklands bridge.

6.2   Here it 'crosses' the later Land Yeo by 2 sluices, and thence proceeds in a slightly higher than natural course to the third group of springs at Moorend Spout. [os.9] [Fig.5] In wet weather its old natural channel can be seen south of the Land Yeo. From here its line continues to Tickenham where it has by now acquired the appellation MIDDLE Yeo. This Yeo once turned north towards Tickenham Church being contained between banks before turning west into a specifically rock-cut ditch in the low limestone batch on which both Church and court stand. The banks were recently thrown down and much of the rock-cut ditch filled, thus diverting the drainage into a lower channel. Before reaching the sea today it loses its identity in a series of cross rhynes and housing estates, (it in fact becomes 'blind' !) [Figs.2-3]. Palaeo-channels on the moor suggest a possible early link with the final , urban stretch of the Land Yeo. [Fig. 3]

7.   The LAND YEO:

7.1   The 'Barrow brook' meanwhile, having fed the mill system at Watercress farm and having re-united with the flow from the mill pond, continues westwards along the north side of Watercress Wood where it forms the boundary between Backwell and Wraxall and, in antiquity, the southern border of Portbury Hundred. [OS.10] **[Fig.7]** At the north west corner of this wood the old Boundary meanders away to follow a hedged ditch which swings to the south west and after two fields joins what seems to be a new stream at Backwell Bow, acknowledged to be the infant KENN RIVER. It is here postulated that in fact the natural source of the Kenn River was the 'Barrow Brook', until its diversion from the Hundredal Boundary into the Land Yeo.

7.2   It would appear that from this north west corner of Watercress Wood the stream diverges from the line of the boundary into a banked waterway which we can now refer to as the LAND YEO. This sweeps in a southerly arc through the northern extremity of Backwell shortly returning to cross the Wraxall boundary line in a north westerly direction. Subsequently it crosses the Little stream to pass the old hunt kennels and the Medieval settlement complex **(Usher 1960)** [OS.11] south east of Wraxall house, where it powered a Mill. Here it rejoins the Little stream under the road and flows along the contour of the valley side below the Roman villa site at Birdcombe (Sykes **1961)** [OS.12] to Jacklands bridge where it is crossed by the infant Middle Yeo, and switches from the south side of the valley to the north side. **[Fig.6]**

7.3   From Jacklands bridge the Land Yeo flows towards Tickenham Church, swings north and then west to feed the Mill at Middleton still maintaining enough head to continue along at a raised elevation. There is a possibility that the Land Yeo took an earlier alternative line south of Tickenham batch via the rock-cut ditch previously mentioned **(6.2)** and that the ditch itself once served a mill south west of the Church **(Walker 1998 f.93)**. Another mill at Clevedon would seem to have been powered by the Land Yeo **[Fig.3]** [OS.13] before it joins the sea at Clevedon Pill, the possible site of a further two (tidal) mills. **(Lilly,J. 1995 p.8) [Fig.2]**

7.4   At no point does this major drainage feature co-incide with any parish or other boundary, unlike the Kenn river and the Parish Brook, a fact perhaps indicative of its relatively late construction. In its final passage to the sea through the built up area of Clevedon it adopts a meandering route and aerial photographic together with early map evidence **(Lilly D. 1991)** suggests that from this point it could well be the natural outlet of the relict Middle Yeo.   There is no evidence that the Land Yeo was cut and embanked at one point in time or as one grand design. In the Birdcombe Valley it would serve well as a water-meadow leat, possibly the work of an early Lord of Wraxall, resident in Birdcombe Court. From Watercress Wood its diversion into Backwell could possibly have been as early as pre-Domesday to power the DB mill. The next section to Wraxall House is closely associated with three potentially datable structures, the Hunt Kennels, the Medieval 'Whelpes Place' (which appears to pre-date it)

[Plate 2.] and the Mill itself. Whatever its purpose it's possibly disjointed origins currently remain an enigma.

8.   The BLIND YEO:

8.1   Returning to Moorend Spout there is a further cut south through the slope of the hill to feed the PARISH BROOK. This maintains a degree of height as Nailsea's old boundary running around the west end of Nailsea Heath and Kingshill to the south side of Tickenham moor to a meerstone, [os.14] before approaching the Kenn river at Nailsea Wall. It is diverted west by the wall and, rejoined the Middle Yeo as the BLIND Yeo, a name which is now formally given to its successor, the 20ft wide new cut opened in the 1950's and which also diverts much of the old Kenn River, (but which is not 'blind'). **[FIG. 4]**

9.   The KENN RIVER:

9.1   This 'yeo', assumed above to have its natural source at Barrow Gurney but generally acknowledged to come at least from Backwell Bow, works its way via the new lake by Nailsea / Backwell railway station, passing a series of spring ponds, and the Domesday holdings of Chelvey **(DB 44.2)** [os.15] and Midgehill **(DB 5.68)** [os.16] It continues south of Nailsea Court and turning north flows to Nailsea Wall, [os.17] all the while serving as the southern boundary of Portbury Hundred. An older serpentine course is still active and is known locally as the Old Yeo Rhyne. Reaching Nailsea Wall it seems to have been diverted west along a cut on the south side of the Wall running parallel to the Blind Yeo and only a matter of feet from it. Here is a now defunct decoy pool system apparently pre-dating the general enclosure lay-out. At Kenn Pier (to which at one time tidal access was supposedly possible) it diverges from its cut course and meanders through the village of Kenn towards the sea at Kingston or 'Sutte' (= South) Pill. **[Fig.9]** Here it originally drained through **Hook's Yere** which was rebuilt in 1684 (**Evans 1983 pp.40-44**) but was straightened into a cut by-pass.* **Note 1.** Now the yere is high and dry, reduced to an isolated piece of walling at the end of a field and the water is channeled through a hatched culvert beneath the field, while the Kenn river ends as a weed covered ditch, its flow diverted into the new Blind Yeo.

10.   The YATTON RIVER:

10.1   The Kenn river was also known as the GREAT RIVER and in contrast there is also a LITTLE RIVER not to be confused with the one in Wraxall. This 'Little' river, referred to in some enclosure maps as the YATTON RIVER serves as an overflow for the Kenn river draining through a sluice [OS.18] west of Nailsea Court, to a series of cuts which in turn drain the wet land north of Claverham and Hillsea. It passes around Stonehurst Batch, and Claverham Common, under Moorstreet Bow and continues westwards passing to the south of the raised ground at Ham Farm with its wetland RB settlement. **(Rippon 1994)** It seems to cut, as Yatton's NW boundary, through a series of Medieval strip fields at Horsecastle Farm called 'Oldfield', and then serves as the north west

---

Note 1. *An engraved stone marking the rebuilding is at present in the keeping of Mr. Gerald Harris at Fairfield Farm, Kingston Seymour.*

boundary of the Wemberham field complex, a DB *pastura* (**DB 6.14 & p.317**) and site of a wetland Roman Villa [OS.19] (**Colebrook-Reade 1855 p.64**) where its earlier course is traced by the Yatton boundary. On **Greenwood's 1822** map it entered the Congresbury Yeo at Danys or Davids Yere [OS.20] but it has since been diverted to exit nearer the estuary at Tuthill's Yere, (**Barraclough 1994**) [OS.21] It is one of two drains to enter the central Congresbury Yeo directly from the northern moors. [**Fig.9**] The other 'yere' draining Kingston Moor south into the main Congresbury Yeo is the Mill Leaze Yere probably the site of a medieval tidal mill, massive timbers having been uncovered there in 1983 (**Evans 1983 p.40-44**) [OS.22]. Recent Carbon 14 analysis suggests a date in the late 12th Century. (**Gardner & Rippon 1998 p.102**) * Note 2.

10.2   In periods of flood a natural meander is visible, marking waterways now known as the Broadstone rhyne and Ham rhyne, which lead towards the mill site. These old waterways emanate from an egg-shaped series of enclosed fields west of Ham Farm, currently identified as 'in-fields', arguably the early pre-Norman farm-steads from which the village grew. (**Gilbert 1996 pp.53-57**) (**Rippon 1996 p.45**) The whole pattern of tight irregular field boundaries in the Kingston Seymour coastal clay belt, is in stark contrast to the straight and regular 18th & 19th century Enclosure Act plots and suggests an early origin for settlement and the control of marine and fresh-water flooding. (**Williams 1970 p.188**)

Note 2.
.We are also indebted to Mr Gerald Harris for drawing our attention to a surviving piece of timber for this purpose.

11.   MAPS.

11.1   Certain evidence for determining the sequential if not absolute dates for the draining of these levels must come from cartographic sources. A primeval and natural system has already been postulated with the Tickenham and Clevedon moors being drained by a **"Middle" Yeo**, and the Kenn and Yatton moors by the **Kenn River**. The northern or **Land Yeo** is almost entirely man made and the southern or **Blind Yeo** even starts with a man-made 'uphill' cut as its point of origin.

11.2.   Early maps of the county are unreliable in their fine detail but the earliest, **Saxton's survey (1575),** shows a two river system commensurate with the above draining to Clevedon Pill and *'Sutte Pyll'*. Aerial photographic evidence supports this interpretation by revealing a network of palaeo-channels. One detail (on which too much reliance should not be placed), is that on all the pre 1782 maps the main drain runs to the south of Tickenham church ostensibly implying that the Land Yeo was not in evidence in the 16th and mid 17th centuries. Late 18th century surveys suggest that the pre-1946 three-Yeo system was largely in place by 1800, supplemented by an improved Kenn River,and with some parts of the system already defunct.

11.3   The major problem with 17th & 18th century county maps is that they all seem to be based on one another. By the time that **Day & Masters** new survey of **1782** was undertaken and published the Clevedon Yeo complex was largely as it is today.

11.4   White's Manorial Survey of Backwell in 1787 shows the northern extremity of the parish isolated by the Land Yeo as now, but with the significant inclusion of a leat and mill [OS.23] **[Fig.10].** The **1810 Ordnance** drawings show a complex of waterways south of Clevedon town which bears little resemblance to those indicated on the **1799 Enclosure** map, but which would be compatible with an earlier stage as shown on Day & Master's. Similar discrepancies of detail in such areas as Tickenham and Wraxall could almost suggest that the OS 1810 was produced in perhaps the 1780's and that, not surprisingly, significant land drainage was part of the Enclosure procedure.

12.   MILLS.

12.1   Domesday mills are 1 at Barrow **(DB5.32)**, 1 at Backwell **(DB 5.30)** and 2 at Wraxall **(DB 5.40)** (not the 'juxta Leigh' one below as that had been built by the donor in late C12 .)

12.2   Of the other sites on the Land Yeo, the earliest implied dates for mills already in existence are: Tickenham 1230 **(Walker 1998 f.93)**, Ashton (Gatcombe) in 1285 **(Dickenson 1889a p.29)**, Clevedon & Bourton in 1327. **(Dickenson 1889b pp 237/9)**

12.3   Mention has been made of a possible tidal mill at Kingston Seymour (c 1175) and two separate sites at Clevedon Pill bear the name Mill Ground on 19th century Tithe maps. **(Lilly J. 1995 p.8)**

12.4   Clevedon and Tickenham have no mills recorded in Domesday but a more positive if confusing piece of evidence is the reference to a possibly defunct cloth Fulling Mill at Clevedon in 1630. A later ground lease (1700) locates this mill in front of Clevedon Court with its southern boundary named as the Land Yeo. The 14th century de Clevedons were involved in cloth commerce and so the Mill and possibly the Land Yeo at this point could be of an early date. The 1630 survey of Clevedon also includes a Mill which to judge by its value was still in operation. (**Lilly J.1995 p.6)**

12.5   The bulk of these observations were committed to paper in 1995; since then however the on-going field and desk-top evaluations have proceeded and there may be some value in elaborating the views stated on three medieval sites in particular, **Tickenham Batch, Wraxall and Backwell Mills.**

12.6   TICKENHAM Batch:

12.6.1 The complex of waterways surrounding the batch on which both Church and Court stand is obviously multiperiod. The most enigmatic feature however is the rock-cut ditch south of the Church . Until the mid 1980's the water from the springs at Moor-end Spout was transported along the Middle Yeo in an embanked channel deliberately to the east end of this rock-cut ditch. Why ? With much less labour the embanked channel could have run around the batch at a lower level. The suggestion is that it wasrequired to maintain height. Was this in order to power a mill ?

12.6.2 The RCHME have now surveyed the earthworks on the batch west of the Court and there also propose the possibility of a mill-site. **(RCHME 1995)**

12.6.3. Roger FitzHarding allowed the church 2/- from the tithes of his mill at Tickenham in the late 12th /early 13th Century. Was this the mill ? (1195 x 1230) **(Walker 1998 f. 93)**

12.6.4 One problem with FitzHarding's mill being the one on the Land Yeo at Middleton is the fact that no such mill is mentioned in either the Obedientary or Manorial Accounts 250 years later. The possibility of a defunct 13th century site being associated with the rock cut ditch south of the Manor cannot be overlooked.

12.6.5 An additional feature which needs to be pursued by geo-physics is a possible interpretation of the Aerial Photograph **(Plate 1)** suggesting that the Land Yeo originally ran directly towards this ditch from the point where it now makes an acute bend to the north-east.

12.7 WRAXALL Mills:

12.7.1 As stated above the natural flow line of the Middle Yeo draining the Backwell – Wraxall valley would take it south of Wraxall House, via an ornamental pond, to power a mill, the case for which is made by **Bodman (1995 p.4.)**

12.7.2. The Land Yeo now takes most of the drainage north of Wraxall House to power the mill there, the site of which is quite apparent. **Bodman (1994 p. 12)**

12.7.3 The obvious remains of what was presumably the *"Whelpe's Place"*referred to in late 14th / early 15th century documents **(Masters 1900 p.35)** would also appear to contain a leat and a pond, pre-dating the Land Yeo which now transects the line of flow. **(Plate 2)** This could be the site of the reference in 1327 to *Ada atte Mulle*. **(SRS.3 p. 236) (Aston & Iles 1986 ? p.104: fig.8.10)**

12.7.4 Wraxall is rated for 2 mills in **Domesday (5.40)** One of these is probably at or near Wraxall House, on the Nailsea border, as Nailsea was apparently part of the Manor of Wraxall and the early Lords of Wraxall lived at Birdcombe Court nearby. The manor also included the present parish of Flax Bourton so the second mill may have been Bourton or Watercress Farm

12.7.5 In Sabin's editing of the 1491/2 Obedientary Accts. of St Augustine **(Sabin 1938 p.94)** he refers in a footnote to a mill included in an early grant as being *"probably on the Yeo near Wraxall."* A later 1511/12 account **(ibid p254)** refers to the mill as being *"Radford juxta Leigh",* and current field research into the foundation grants shows this to be at a hitherto unrecognized Medieval Settlement at Radford–juxta–Leigh where Failand's boundary with Abbots Leigh is, for 600 metres, the Markham Brook. This mill was built by Richard de Radford by 1199 **(Gardner 1996 p.5) (Walker 1998 f. 296)** [qv : matching Manorial Accounts in **Sabin 1960**]

12.8   BACKWELL Mill.

12.8.1 Backwell is credited with 1 mill in **DB (5.30)** There is only one traditional site of a mill in the parish and that is on the Land Yeo west of Watercress Wood. It was subject to a law suit in c.1270. **(SRS. 6 p.227 & 36 p. 22)** The possibility is that the Land Yeo was cut for this purpose at this point and early estate maps **(Fig.10)** indicate a now levelled leat where the 1st Edition OS 1" shows an 'Old Mill'. The Aerial Photograph **(Plate 3)** shows a veritable labyrinth of palaeo-channels to the east of the mill site, which could well represent an earlier water-power system.

12.8.2 A notable feature here is that the Hundred boundary continues along a meandering hedge ditch, ostensibly the original stream, whilst the new Land Yeo sweeps in an arc to service the mill site within the manor's land. **[Fig.7]**

12.8.2 A corresponding situation interestingly exists in the relationship between Watercress Mill and the Hundred boundary east of Watercress Wood.

13   DRAINAGE REPORTS.

13.1 Traditionally authority for the drainage of the area was vested in the Wrington Commissioner of Sewers, under whom sat the Yatton Jury. There is little in their reports which throws light on the piecemeal development of the landscape, but they give a good insight into the day to day administration of the drainage system. There was for example a fine for driving any waggon on Kenn Moor Wall;

rhynes had to be keetched *"by Lady Day next, against a penalty of 2d per rope in default."* The Decoyman was instructed under penalty *"not to cut through the banks of any of the several Rivers Yeo to let water into the decoy or into Kenn Moor."*

13.2   The Yatton Jury of Sewers Reports are at Taunton (SRO) reference **D/RA/1/2/ 120-124** dated 1774-1937. Ref: **D/RA 1/2 37 & 38** are schedules and a plan relating to the Land Yeo in 1854

14.   ENCLOSURE AWARDS

14.1   These, such as they are, merely confirm a late and piecemeal development of the rhyne system, and it is not always clear whether or not these were incorporated into an earlier YEO network. In 1749 for example the Common land north of Claverham Court was enclosed, with the Yatton or Little River as its northern boundary. This merely indicates that this main drain was in existence at that time and not that it was constructed for the purpose. **(Barraclough 1991 p.55)**

15.   CHURCHWARDENS ACCOUNTS

15.1   Accounts for 1548 from Yatton contain a useful reference to *"ye makyng of a sirten sklusse or yere agenste the rage of ye salte water, called Danys Yere,set and beyng yn West Wemerham,the which yere then beying ruynus and yn dekay"* **(Hobhouse 1890 p.160)** This is the early outfall of the Yatton or Little River and was so until 1846, when a 'new cut' moved the outfall to the west further downstream.

16.   DOMESDAY: [All references are to the Phillimore 1980 Edition]

16.1   Phillimore postulates **(DB 5.29& p353)** that Kenn was once within the Hundred of Portbury, suggesting that an earlier course of the Kenn River would have needed to run south of the village. There is evidence of this in the shape of meandering rhynes and palaeo-channels. By 1347 Kenn was in Winterstoke Hundred . Saxton's and Speed's 16th / 17th century maps show Kenn church as being situated north of the Kenn River and not south of it as it is today, although this position may be purely symbolic

16.2   Most Domesday manors bordering the levels have sufficient dry land to hold their gelded acreage. Two manors totally in floodable land however are those of Kingston Seymour, whose geldage suggests a form of priveleged hidage or 'rate rebate'- perhaps for drainage and maintenance of the sea-walls ? **(DB 5.63 / 64)**

17.   AERIAL PHOTOGRAPHS (CPE/UK 1869.)

17.1   A good impression of the state of the primeval peat marshes of Tickenham and Kenn Moors can be obtained from the 1946 series of Air Ministry surveys. The state of agricultural tenure 50 years ago when these were taken, allowed a number of features to be far more prominent than they might be today, particularly the network of 'palaeo-channels' or old river systems. These, many of which have since been ploughed down, give the impression of a network of meandering delta like water courses merging and diverging so that one can well imagine it as a "deep and morassy" wasteland. The vertical view however not only gives some indication of the early courses of the Yeo complex but reveals enigmatic straight lines, crop-marks and shadows presumably representing early attempts to improve the drainage by linking different water courses. Whether this phase was medieval or even Romano-British is as yet unclear but it seems to pre-date the enclosure period and the existing Land, Middle and Blind Yeos. (For extant examples see **Lilly.D.1991**)

18. LITERARY REFERENCES

18.1 Early descriptive comments give some indication of the state of the North Marsh in the 16th to 18th centuries.

18.2 Leland 1543. *"Banwell stands not very wholesome and Wike* worse. The fens be almost at hand "*
(* WIKE, referred to as being the residence of the Newtons was probably Court de Wyck at Claverham near Yatton, not Wick St Lawrence as generally claimed)

18.3 Collinson 1791 *"a large moor,deep and morassy and two centuries ago impassable" (ie 1590's)*

18.4 Billingsley 1797 *".......the North Marsh, the present state of which is disgraceful to the owners..."*

18.5 There is an interesting 13th century reference to a deed whereby **Nicholas FitzRoger** (ob. 1262) grants to the Hospital of St..Marks the right of digging peat on his moor of Tickenham and of cutting and collecting sedges and rushes,provided that – *" they shall not despoil his or his heirs crops or meadow if through his industry or that of his* *(heirs) the moor should be brought into cultivation or converted to meadow ."* (**Ross 1959 p.262**)

19. LOCAL HISTORICAL SOCIETIES

19.1   These have tended to operate on a somewhat parochial basis but have nevertheless carried out research which has added much detail to the outline. Clevedon, Backwell, Nailsea and Yatton / Kingston Seymour (as well as Banwell and Congresbury south of the Congresbury Yeo) all have working groups that have produced excellent reports on various local aspects of the problems without addressing the wider overall question of the network origins.

20.   SUMMARY.

20.1   The initial aim of this survey has been to present an historical outline of currently drained areas north of the Congresbury Yeo. A similar survey is under way for the area south of that river.

20.2   The area under study here is one with much archaeological and historical potential. Lower and Upper Palaeolithic are well represented from gravel and from inter-tidal sites, as are a Mesolithic structure and examples of preserved early timberwork. The wetland Roman villa contained in a named Domesday *pastura* is probably unique whilst the peripheral site of Cadbury /Congresbury is of national significance. Documentary evidence, whilst by no means complete is promising; some of the earliest Church Accounts are from Yatton, and the co-incidence of having both the Obedientary and Manorial Monastic Accounts for the same year should prove invaluable.

20.3   A SEQUENCE ?   As a purely working hypothesis we might have:

20.3.1   A primeval Early Iron Age (?) marshland with no sea defences or engineered drainage systems.

20.3.2   By 2nd Century sea and river defences were sufficiently developed to allow the investment in a substantial and sophisticated building at Wemberham.

20.3.3   At the same time marginal land on the inner edge of the clay belt was drainable to an extent that made it capable of being farmed .

20.3.4   Apart from the Sub-Roman activity implied by the re-occupation of Cadbury there is no direct evidence of the state or use of these levels for this time. However deposits of alluvium in the later RB ditches at Kenn suggest an innundation which may possibly have rendered the levels uninhabitable by the 5th Century.

20.3.5   By late Saxon times not only had the villa site at Wemberham become a named pastura in Domesday, but two comparitively wealthy manors at Kingston were sited on wetland clay, now totally dependant on drains and dykes. Settlements of the period are still recognizable in the field as 'egg-shaped' bundles of enclosures.

20.3.6   Two, if not three Domesday mills are likely to be near the Land Yeo, ie Backwell's well referenced site which appears on maps until c.1800, and one at least of Wraxall's. The Barrow Brook seems to have been diverted to become the Land Yeo specifically to have powered a Backwell mill within the manor, but there seem to be vestiges of an earlier system there. The Wraxall House complex probably contains a mill site earlier than the one extant in the 17th Century, powered by the ornamental pool to the south west of the house. Was this the earliest ?

20.3.7   By the mid-13th Cent local landowners are referring to the possibility of reclaiming Tickenham peat moor to meadowland, and it may well be to this or the next century that we should look for the Birdcombe water meadows and the construction of Nailsea Wall, as the Meer Wall and the Wow Wall would seem to have been in use in the 14th century

20.3.8   The Deserted Medieval Settlement's system of leats appears to have been cut across by the Land Yeo which would therefore date that waterway as 15th C or later.

20.3.9   Church warden Accounts for Yatton of 1548 refer to repairing or replacing the already decayed Danys Yere. This was at the exit of the Yatton River into the Congresbury Yeo. Such a 'yere' would have been required, one would have thought to make either the Villa or the DB *pastura* viable !

20.3.10   Monastic involvement in the area may well have promoted drainage through to the 16th century,and historical evidence is available for the existence of some form of the Yeo complex by mid-17th Cent. The straight cuts linking old palaeo-channels seems to be early pre-enclosure attempts at drainage, but how early ? Could they be RB ?

20.3.11   From Day & Master's and the subsequent Enclosure and Tithe Maps,we have well mapped layouts not dis-similar to that existing today with the peculiar exception of the anachronistic OS drawings dated as 1810

20.4   Concluding Comments:

20.4.1   The last 50 years or so has witnessed much change in agriculture, in drainage and inevitably in the landscape itself. No longer can one skate from Tickenham to Yatton across the frozen flood. The old land, arguably unaltered since Enclosure has been fortuitously fossilized by the Aerial Photographic survey of 1946.

20.4.2   Studies continue on various aspects of the history and archaeology of the drainage of the North Marsh. This paper has been published as an interim framework and to serve as a base for more intensive field work and in-depth documentary research by students of Landscape Archaeology.

📖 ksg.11/98

APPENDIX 1:

Some pre-Roman Wetland Sites.

1.) Lower Palaeolithic Acheulian Hand Axes ST/ 424 698 C.M.Sykes: in gravel spoil during construction of new 'Blind Yeo' (Photos with C&DAS)

2.) Upper Palaeolithic Creswellian (?) flint assemblage ST/ 385 702 C.M.Sykes: inter-tidal site Blackstone Rocks. Also Neolithic /Bronze AgeRef. UBSS Vol 5, No.1 1938

3) Mesolithic. Podsolized floor & microliths ST/ 475 718 C.M.Sykes: Site based on 'Whirly Pools' spring on natural drainage line at Birdcombe. Microliths also obtained from gravel bed of spring. Ref. SNANHS. Vol 104 p 106 1960 Additional excavations carried out by Paula Gardiner.(Bristol;Ph.D.research)1997. Report forthcoming.

4.) Neolithic / Bronze Age Preserved carved wood.   ST/ 439 694   Trenching produced worked wood from peat layers c4,000-3500 BP SANHS Vol 127 ;1983 p.1 - 6

5.) Iron Age /RB. Stone Causeway - Glastonbury ware. ST/ 438 715 J.Gray Usher: EIA pottery in and between stone slabs, overlaid by 3rd/4th C wares, all under layer of blue clay. (KSG Archive notes)

6) Iron Age (?) Human Burial in Peat. ST / 457 713 Pipelaying in 1956 exposed burial, crouched 5 ft.deep in peat on Tickenham Moor.(Skull with C&DAS)

APPENDIX 2:

National Grid Refs.

1.	Barrow Tanks	ST 535 675
2.	Gatcombe RB	ST 526 699
3.	Watercress Farm	ST 500 706
4.	Wraxall House	ST 485 715
5.	Jacklands Bridge	ST 470 715
6.	Tickenham Mill	ST 454 717
7.	Clevedon Pill	ST 390 702
8.	'Sutte Pyll'	ST 383 688
9.	Moorend Spout	ST 466 715
10.	Watercress Wood	ST 497 704
11.	Wraxall Kennels/DMV	ST 488 713
12.	Wraxall Villa	ST 478 716
13.	Court Mill	ST 423 714
14.	Meerstone	ST 458 706
15.	Chelvey	ST 466 684
16.	Midghill	ST 461 680
17.	Nailsea Wall	ST 440 694
18.	Stile Sluice	ST 449 680
19.	Wemberham	ST 405 652
20.	Danys Yere	ST 395 663
21.	Tuthill's Yere	ST 381 658
22.	Mill Leaze Yere	ST 378 663
23	Backwell Mill	ST 494 703
	(and relict leat on Land Yeo)	

☐

BIBLIOGRAPHY:

(NB. All Domesday references are from the Phillimore edition and give section and item numbers as per Somerset volume.)

Aston M. & Iles R.	1986	Archaeology of Avon. ACC
Barraclough M.	1991	History of Yatton YLHS
Billingsley,J.	1797	Agriculture of Somerset
Branigan,K.	1977	Gatcombe. BAR 44
Bodman,M.	1994	Mills on the Land Yeo No 1 NDLHS
CADREX	1991	Cadbury Congresbury BAR 223
Collinson,J.	1791	History of Somerset
Coward,H.	1980	SANHS Vol. 183 .
Colebrook-Reade	1855	SANHS Vol 31.
Dickenson F.H.	1889a	SRS 3 Kirby's Quest 1285
Dickenson F.H.	1889b	SRS.3 Exchequer Lay Subsidies 1327
Evans,J.	1983	BAAS 2.
Forrest,D.	1975	The Making of a Manor
Gardiner P.	1998>>>	Doctoral Thesis (forthcoming)
Gardner K.S.	1985	BAAS 4.
Gardner K.S.	1977	In Branigan 1977.
Gardner K.S.	1996	Pennant No 14
Gardner & Rippon	1997	SELRC 7
Hobhouse,Bishop	1890	SRS 4 Churchwardens Account
Leland, J.	1543	The Itinerary (S. Illinois Uni.)
Lilly,D.	1991	Early River Systems CCS
Lilly,J.	1995	Mills on the Land Yeo No2 NDLHS
Masters G.S.	1900	Parochial History of Wraxall SANHS 1900
Rippon,S.	1994	Kenn Moor SELRC 5 pp.21-34
Rippon S	1995	Kenn Moor SELRC 6 pp.35-47
Rippon S.	1996	Banwell & Puxton SELRC 7 pp.39-52
Rippon S.	1997	Banwell & Puxton SELRC 8. pp 41-54
Rippon S.	1997a	The Severn Estuary Leicester U.P.
Ross C.D.	1959	BRS XXI. (St.Marks Cartulary)
RCHME	1995	Ref: UID 195294
Sabin,A.	1938	BRS IX (Obedientary Accts. St.Augustines)
Sabin,A.	1960	BRS XXII (Manorial Accts. St.Augustines)
Sykes, C.M.	1938	UBSS Vol.5 No 1.
Sykes, C.M.	1960	SANHS Vol. 104 .
Sykes,C..M.	1961	SANHS Vol. 105
Usher,J.Gray	1960	Clevedon Mercury Jan. 9th 1960
Walker, D.	1998	B&GAS Cartulary of St Augustines Abbey
Williams, M.	1970	Draining of the Somerset Levels Cantab U.P.

ABBREVIATIONS:

BAAS	Bristol & Avon Archaeological Society
B&GAS	Bristol & Gloucestershire Archaeological Society
BAR	British Archaeological Research papers.
BRS	Bristol Record Society
C&DAS	Clevedon & District Archaeological Society
CCS	Clevedon Civic Society.
NDLHS	Nailsea & District Local History Society
RCHME	Royal Commission: Historical Monuments, England
SANHS	Somerset Archaeological & Natural History Society
SELRC	Severn Estuary Levels Research Committee
SRS	Somerset Record Society
UBSS	University of Bristol Spaeleological Society
YLHS	Yatton Local History Society

It would be appreciated if Research Students would, as a matter of courtesy, kindly contact such institutions as may seem relevant to the areas in which they propose to operate.

Secretaries of these institutions, and others not listed will be pleased to give every assistance to those who are interested in carrying out field-work.

The Council for British Archaeology
will provide contact addresses. They may be contacted at:

**Bowes Morrell House,
111 Walmgate St.,
York, YO1 2UA.   Tel 01 904 671417**

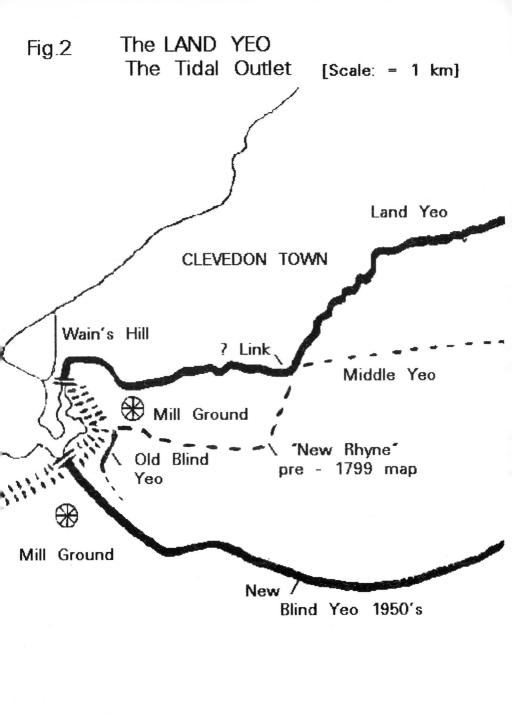

Fig.2   The LAND YEO
         The Tidal Outlet   [Scale: = 1 km]

Land Yeo

CLEVEDON TOWN

Wain's Hill

? Link

Middle Yeo

Mill Ground

Old Blind
Yeo

"New Rhyne"
pre - 1799 map

Mill Ground

New

Blind Yeo 1950's

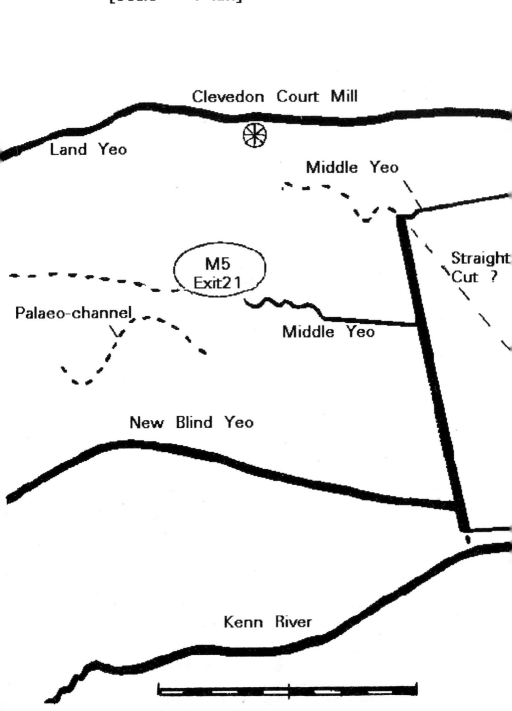

Fig.3 The LAND YEO: Clevedon Moor
[Scale = 1 km]

Clevedon Court Mill

Land Yeo

Middle Yeo

M5
Exit21

Straight
Cut ?

Palaeo-channel

Middle Yeo

New Blind Yeo

Kenn River

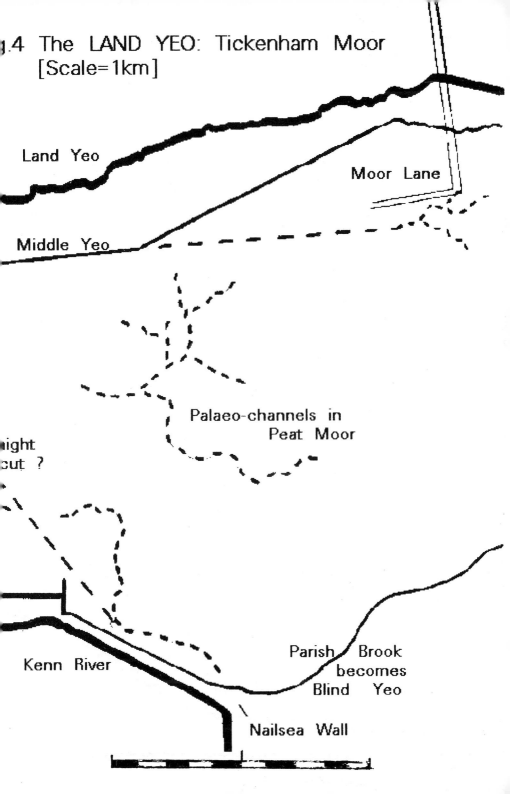

4 The LAND YEO: Tickenham Moor
   [Scale=1km]

Land Yeo

Moor Lane

Middle Yeo

Palaeo-channels in
Peat Moor

ight
cut ?

Parish Brook
becomes
Blind Yeo

Kenn River

Nailsea Wall

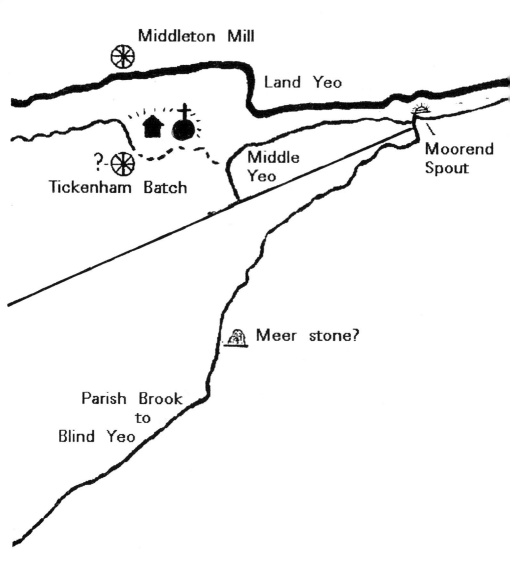

Middleton Mill

Land Yeo

Tickenham Batch

Middle
Yeo

Moorend
Spout

Meer stone?

Parish Brook
to
Blind Yeo

Fig.5 The LAND YEO:
Tickenham Batch and
Nailsea Parish Brook
(Scale = 1 Km.)

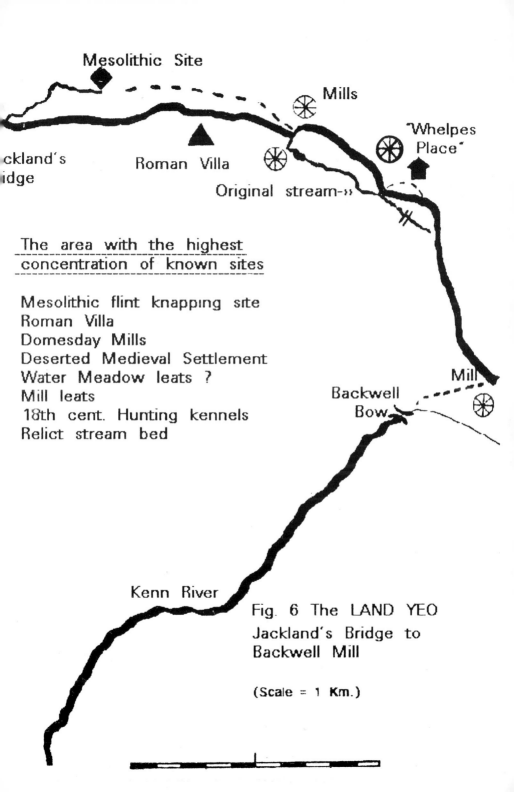

Mesolithic Site

Mills

"Whelpes Place"

ckland's idge

Roman Villa

Original stream→

The area with the highest
concentration of known sites

Mesolithic flint knapping site
Roman Villa
Domesday Mills
Deserted Medieval Settlement
Water Meadow leats ?
Mill leats
18th cent. Hunting kennels
Relict stream bed

Backwell Bow

Mill

Kenn River

Fig. 6 The LAND YEO
Jackland's Bridge to
Backwell Mill

(Scale = 1 Km.)

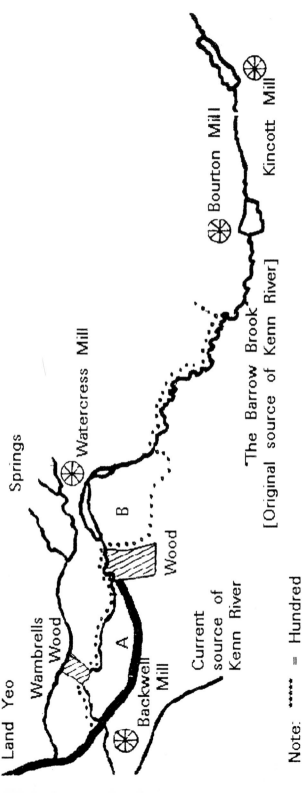

Land Yeo

Springs

Wambrells Wood

Watercress Mill

A

B

Wood

Backwell Mill

Current source of Kenn River

The Barrow Brook
[Original source of Kenn River]

Bourton Mill

Kincott Mill

Note: ***** = Hundred Boundary=old streams ?

A & B are parts of 2 old Manors isolated by diversion of streams to serve their respective mills

Fig.7 The LAND YEO Backwell Mill to Kincott Mill

(Scale = 1 Km.)

Fig.8 The LAND YEO /"Barrow Brook" Barrow Gurney via Gatcombe Roman Settlement to Mill

Scale:= 1km

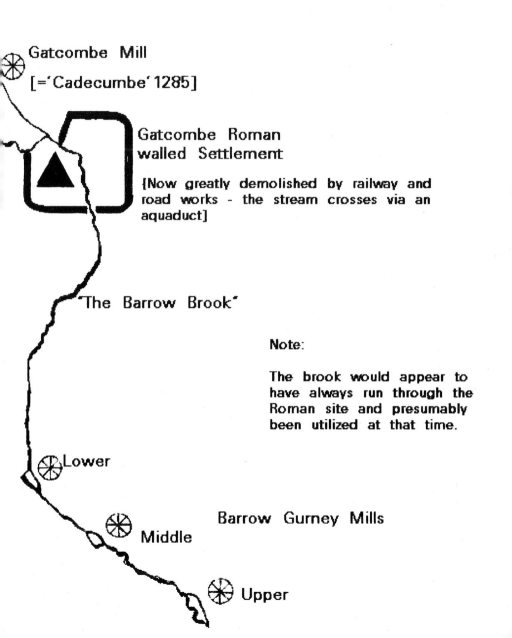

Gatcombe Mill

[='Cadecumbe' 1285]

Gatcombe Roman walled Settlement

[Now greatly demolished by railway and road works - the stream crosses via an aquaduct]

"The Barrow Brook"

Note:

The brook would appear to have always run through the Roman site and presumably been utilized at that time.

Lower

Barrow Gurney Mills

Middle

Upper

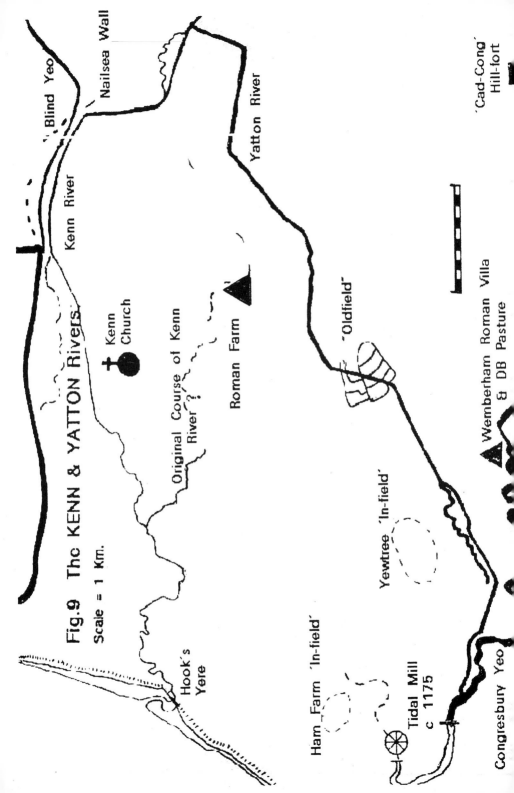

Fig.9 The KENN & YATTON Rivers

Scale = 1 Km.

Blind Yeo

Nailsea Wall

Yatton River

Kenn River

Kenn Church

Original Course of Kenn River?

Roman Farm

Hook's Yere

'Oldfield'

'Cad-Cong' Hill-fort

Wemberham Roman Villa & DB Pasture

Yewtree 'In-field'

Ham Farm 'In-field'

Tidal Mill c 1175

Congresbury Yeo

Fig.10

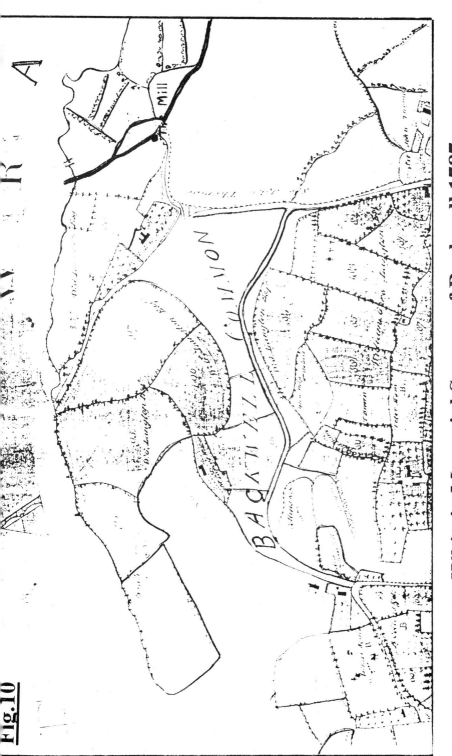

White's Manorial Survey of Backwell 1787.
Note Mill-site on Land Yeo and now vanished leat

(With Acknowledgements to the Marquis of Bath)

The Wraxall Mill Sites:

"Whelpe's Place" DMV/ ? Mill @ Wraxall

(Enlargement ex RAF 4076 – Note relict mill-leat; kennels bottom right)

Tickenham Batch:

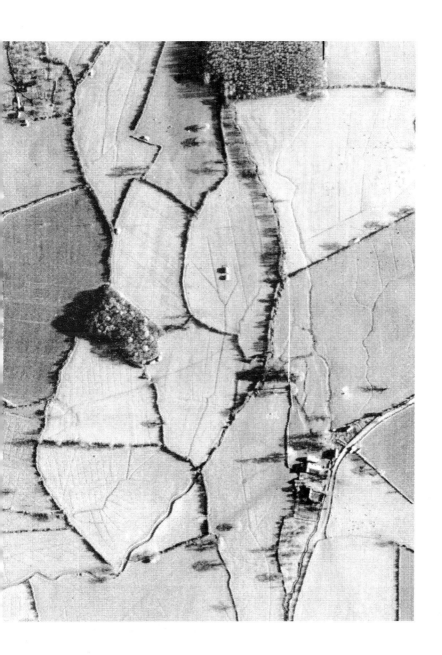

Backwell Mill Site:
(RAF - 3080)

Publications of Nailsea and District Local History Society (N&DLHS) & Others available from its Secretary.

WARTIME

Villages at War: Backwell, Nailsea, Tickenham and Wraxall 1939 - 1945		£3.50 inc p&p
Peace for our Time Backwell, Nailsea, Tickenham and Wraxall 1939 - 1945		£3.50 inc p&p

NEWSPAPERS

Nailsea Village News - Further Newspaper Accounts of life in Victorian times		£1.50 inc p&p

BOOKS ABOUT SURROUNDING PARISHES

Mills on the Land Yeo	Pennant Special No 1	£2.00 inc p&p
Mills on the Land Yeo - Further Discoveries	Pennant Special No 2	£2.00 inc p&p
A Short History of Chelvey	Pennant Special No 3	£2.50 inc p&p

PAROCHIAL RECORDS

Holy Trinity Churchyard, Nailsea: Tombstone Inscriptions 1978	Nailsea Records No 1	£3.00 inc p&p
Nailsea Parochial School - Admissions Register 1877 - 1911	Nailsea Records No 2	£6.50 inc p&p

PEOPLE AND PLACES

Nailsea Village Institute and Church House	People and Places No 1	£3.00 inc p&p
Youngwood Lane, Nailsea An Historical Landscape - well worth exploring	People and Places No 2	£1.00 inc p&p
Backwell The 1891 Census - Some Observations with alphabetical name index	People and Places No 3	£5.00 inc p&p
Nailsea Tannery	People and Places No 4	£1.50 inc p&p
Wraxall Court - near Bristol	People and Places No 5	£3.50 inc p&p

BOOKS BY MARGARET THOMAS

The Nailsea Glassworks		£4.00 inc p&p
The Nailsea Coalmines		£4.00 inc p&p
Nailsea		£4.00 inc p&p

Nailsea - a Handbook of Dates and Events (from prehistory to 1997)	Scene from the Past No 1	£6.50 inc p & p

SOCIETY JOURNAL

PENNANT the local history journal of Backwell Nailsea Tickenham & Wraxall.   Published each January, May, September

UK Subscription per calendar year £7.00 inc. p & p   Sets of 21 Journals issued to & inc. 1998 available £25 inc. p&p

The Secretary N&DLHS c/o 5 The Perrings Nailsea Bristol BS48 4YD. Tel No 01275 852993. Send SAE for membership details.

All Prices shown include postage and packing for up to three items. For multiple purchases or trade contact Secretary N&DLHS